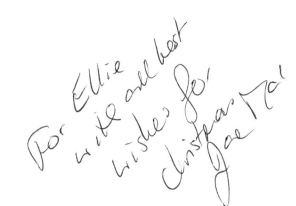

For Ellie with all best wishes for Christmas Jae M.

Sammy, The Squirrel Who Missed Christmas

Written By Jae Malone
Illustrations by Jess Hawksworth

Other books in this series of animal stories for younger children
With illustrations by Jess Hawksworth

Lorna and the Loch Ness Monster
The Raven and the Thief
Blue Teaches A Lesson
Mrs Pringles Needs A Nurse
Tib and Tab Make A Friend

Books for older children (from nine to ninety-nine)
The Winterne Series
Silver Linings
Queen of Diamonds
Fool's Gold
Avaroc Returns

And linked to the Winterne Series but standalone historical novel:
From Knight to Knave

Acknowledgements

Recognising the wonderful work Forests and Land Scotland do in managing the green areas of Scotland, and the massive contribution to the continuing success of forestry in Scotland. Work on the national forests and land adds £1 million to the Scottish economy each day, supports 11,000 jobs, soaks up over three million tonnes of CO_2 each year and hosts over eighty community projects with a focus on inclusive activities.

My thanks to Jess Hawksworth again for her beautiful illustrations. This is the sixth very happy collaboration between us, even though Jess has been working hard on her Masters degree. Hopefully we still have at least two more books in the series to come. More news on that in due course.

Thank you too, to New Generation Publishing. In particular the Managing Director, Daniel Cooke, and his team David Walshaw, Lauren, Saskia and Sam Rennie. Daniel has been my publisher since 2005 and I rely on NGP totally.

Sammy, The Squirrel Who Missed Christmas

Just outside a town in Scotland called Dumfries, stands Mabie Forest, a vast woodland  of pine trees, ancient oaks and lots of other types of tree. There visitors can see splendid views of the River Nith, and Dalshinnie Loch. If you ever go to Mabie Forest, you might be lucky enough to see some of the wonderful animals who live there. One of these animals is Sammy, the red squirrel.

Little Sammy had made a cosy nest in hole in a tree trunk that had been made by Woodpeckers. They lived in the forest as well and each year they made holes in the tree trunks with their beaks to make a nest. When their babies grow up and fly away, the parents leave the nest and build a new one the following year. So, if you're ever in a forest and you hear a tap-tap-tapping sound, it may be a woodpecker making another nest.

Sammy was lucky enough to find one of these empty holes in the trunk of a pine tree, and it was big enough to make a very good home for him.

Pine trees are different to many other types of trees, as they do not lose their leaves in the autumn. The pine tree where Sammy lived had not only kept most of its leaves – called needles because they're long and quite sharp – but it was in the middle of several closely packed trees that sheltered Sammy's nest from the icy winds in the winter months.

Another very good thing about Sammy's tree was that it still had lots of seed-filled cones growing on it. The seeds were very good for Sammy, and he had plenty of cones close to his nest. But sometimes he wanted a change, so he had little hidden stores with other types of food, such as acorns and berries nearby.

One morning Sammy awoke, stretched, licked his front paws to wash behind his ears, brushed his bushy tail with his fingers, and then went out to get his breakfast. It was just as he was going outside, he remembered it was a very special day, but he couldn't recall what was special about it. 'Oh well, I expect it will come to me later,' he said. When he stepped outside he had a nasty surprise. The trees and the ground were all covered in white after a blustery snow storm during the night. Broken branches lay scattered about, and the last leaves on the branches on all except the pine trees, had all gone leaving uncovered boughs and twigs. Sammy had slept so soundly, he hadn't heard the storm at all. But now the wind had softened to a gentle breeze, and the pale yellow sun cast soft bands of sparkling gold where it touched the ground between the trees. It was a crisp and cold, but beautiful morning.

Sammy heard someone crying and saw a pair of robins sitting on a nearby branch and it was Mrs Robin who was sobbing. Mr Robin wrapped his wing around her and nodded a sad greeting to Sammy.

'What's the matter?' Sammy asked him. Mrs Robin cried even more loudly.

'The storm blew our nice warm nest away and we won't have time to build a new home before night time. My wife is frightened of what might happen to us in the dark.'

Sammy thought for a moment, then he smiled and said: 'There's an opening in the trunk of my tree, just a little higher up. It's not very big but it might make a good shelter for you both until you can build something better, and I could help you find leaves to make it more comfortable if you like, and I think I know where to find a bit of badger hair where they scratch against trees. Would that help?'

Mrs Robin stopped crying. 'Oh, that would be so good of you. Thank you, Sammy. I was so scared of being outside at night time. It's so cold.'

'You'll find the opening two branches up,' Sammy told Mrs Robin. 'You stay there and keep warm while Mr Robin and I go to find things to make it more comfortable for you.'

Sammy scrambled up and down the tree trunk lots and lots of times, carrying damp leaves, old feathers and some hair he thought had come from a fox tail. Mr Robin brought small twigs and green moss he had picked off stones, and soon Mrs Robin was all smiles. Mr Robin even found some beetle grubs under the moss and took them back for their dinner. They both thanked Sammy and snuggled into their safe new home where they could keep warm until a new and more sturdy home could be built.

After spending so much time helping the robins, Sammy, who still hadn't had his breakfast was starving. 'Oh dear,' he said, 'my tummy's rumbling. I'll have to go and find something to eat.' He wrapped his tail around his neck to help keep himself warm and scurried down the tree trunk to find one of his larders. He had some acorns, hazelnuts, blackberries, pine cones and even some mushrooms stored in holes in tree trunks and in the ground.

After a few minutes of scraping away snow, earth and leaves, Sammy uncovered one of his buried stores and was just about to bite into one of the acorns when he heard the sound of little feet scampering towards him across the snow. He quickly hid the acorn under the snow and spun around ready to fight anyone who might be trying to steal his food, but a moment later he smiled. It wasn't anyone to be scared of. It was his older sister, Susie, but she looked very sad.

Sammy ran over to her: 'Oh, Susie! You scared me creeping up on me like that. What's wrong?'

Susie burst into tears and through her sobs she told him; 'Did you hear that strong wind last night?'

Sammy shook his head. 'No, I slept right through it. I've just helped Mr and Mrs Robin find somewhere to stay after their nest was blown away.

'Well, it's broken up my lovely nest too,' she cried, 'and it's Christmas Eve...'

'Ah, that's what it is,' said Sammy. 'I knew it was a special day but...'

'Yes, but what am I going to do, Sammy. It was my home and it was warm and comfortable, and all my soft bedding blew away. I have nowhere to live.'

'I did wonder whether your nest would be safe in an oak tree.' Sammy said. 'It was only made of moss, leaves and twigs and squashed in between two branches. I did say I thought it might blow away in a strong wind.'

'…But oak trees are so strong,' said Susie. 'I thought it would be safe on an oak tree branch,' Susie whimpered.

'Yes, but oak trees lose all their leaves in the winter, so your nest had nothing to protect it from bad weather.' He put his arm around Susie. 'Look, I've got an idea. I've just found some leaves and feathers, and even hair from a fox's tail for Mr and Mrs Robin to line their new nest with, but I got too much and have some left over. There are fields nearby with sheep in them and sometimes some of the wool gets caught on the wire. There's a pine tree next to mine that has an empty hole that would make a really safe nest for you…and it won't blow away.'

Susie looked up at him through tear-dropped eyelashes: 'Would you really do that, Sammy? It would be so good of you. I was really worried about how I was going to keep warm tonight.'

While Susie looked for soft things to make her new nest warm and cosy, Sammy scurried up the tree he had told Susie about to see if the hole there really would make a good home for her. He found it very high up, close to where two strong branches grew close together, and the entrance faced south so the cold north wind would not blow in. Inside there was a little hallway that sloped upward to another larger room. Susie would be comfortable there. It would be warm and dry; very little rain would get inside the upper room, and when it was full of soft, warm leaves and hair it would be cosy. This was the one.

From high up on the wide branch he called down to Susie. 'This would be perfect for you, Susie. Come and have a look.'

Carefully hiding everything she had gathered together in case another squirrel stole it, Susie scampered up the trunk of the tree to where Sammy was waiting for her. She peered into the opening. 'You're sure there's no-one in here?' she asked.

'No. There's no-one living here. I've been inside,' Sammy told her. 'You'll be safe and warm and it's not far from my home. Go inside and take a look.'

Susie disappeared inside and two minutes later she came back out with a huge smile on her face. 'Oh, Sammy. It's perfect. Thank you for finding it.'

'Come on,' said Sammy with a swish of his tail. 'Let's bring all your nesting up, make the place comfortable and then find you some food.'

Soon after, Sammy waved goodbye to Susie as she settled herself into her new home with enough food to last her until the next day. At long last he could finally get his breakfast. He was even more hungry now and, after all the running about he was feeling a bit tired.

But as Sammy ran down the trunk of his tree to collect a blackberry he had saved, he met his grandfather, Sidney. Sidney was leaning on his walking stick and frowning, he looked rather puzzled.

'Hello, Grandpa,' said Sammy. 'What's the matter? You look lost.'

Sidney turned to Sammy and seemed even more confused. 'Who...? Oh, it's you...um... Sammy. For a moment there I couldn't remember who you were and, yes, please, I could use your help.'

Sammy frowned. That wasn't like his grandfather at all. 'Yes it's me, Grandpa. Are you looking for something?'

'Hmm. Aye. I can't remember where my larders are and I'm hungry.'

'Well, why don't we look for them together, Grandpa?' asked Sammy, gently.

'You're a good boy, Sammy,' said Sidney. 'Thank you.'

Sometime later, Sammy found one of Sidney's larders buried under snow and leaves, at the bottom of a tall and wide oak tree trunk. Sidney was delighted, but then, try as he might, he couldn't remember where his nest was. Thankfully, Sammy knew, and led the elderly squirrel back to his cosy home where he left him safe and warm with enough food to keep Sidney well fed for a few days. It was on his way home that Sammy realised he and Susie would need to make sure Sidney was well looked after from then on.

Helping Mr and Mrs Robin, Susie and Grandpa Sidney had taken so much time that the sun was setting, and the moon was rising in the darkening sky. Sammy was cold, very hungry and awfully tired. He plodded back to where he had left his uneaten acorn, held it

in his teeth and wearily climbed to his nest. The other food he was going to dig up could wait but just outside the entrance of his nest, he left the acorn for a moment to find a nice thick pine cone.

Inside, now lovely and warm, Sammy, tried hard to keep his eyes open while he slowly munched on the pine cone seeds. He was too tired to crunch through the shell of the acorn. That could wait until later, but first he needed a nap. Soon after, curling his tail around him to keep warm, Sammy fell asleep.

When he awoke, feeling much better, Sammy had a breakfast of the acorn and the left over pine seeds. He looked outside. It was another beautiful, cold and crisp day.

As he ran down to the ground Susie called out; 'Happy Boxing Day, Sammy.'

'Boxing Day? 'No, it's Christmas Day,' said Sammy. 'You're playing a trick on me. It's Christmas Day and we get presents today. I'm looking forward to seeing Santa Claus when he comes to see us.' Then Sammy noticed something. 'What's that you're wearing?' Susie had a lovely green woolly scarf around her neck.

'No, Sammy. It really is Boxing Day. Santa came yesterday. You slept a whole day and missed Santa Claus. This scarf was my present from him.'

Just then Grandpa Sidney appeared. He was wearing a pair of sheepskin lined boots. 'Santa gave me these to keep my feet and legs warm,' he told Sammy.

Sammy sat down on a tree stump and shook his head. He just couldn't believe it. He didn't understand how he could possibly have slept for so long.

At that moment a sound of jingling bells came from within the forest. The sound grew louder and louder as it approached to where Sammy and his companions were standing. Imagine their surprise as a wonderful red and gold sleigh, being pulled by eight reindeer, emerged from the trees and stopped right in front of Sammy.

Santa Claus smiled down at Sammy and reached behind him for a small parcel, wrapped in blue paper with gold stars and a big gold bow. He stepped out of the sleigh and walked up to a very surprised Sammy. Just then, Mr and Mrs Robin flew down from the pine tree and settled on the antlers of one of the leading reindeer.

'Sammy, our dear little Sammy,' Santa Claus said, his loud voice echoing through the forest, 'after all the help you gave those in need on Christmas Eve, I couldn't forget you, now could I? I wasn't going to let you be the one squirrel who missed Christmas when you had done so much for others. So, here's a little present for you, from me.'

Too astonished to speak, Sammy unwrapped the paper and opened the box. Inside was a little blue woollen jacket with gold stars and a matching bobble hat. He smiled, took them out and Susie helped him put them on. Sammy looked up at Santa Claus. 'Thank you so much, Santa. They're lovely and it was so good of you to come to see me.'

'My pleasure, my boy, but now I must go. I have next Christmas to start thinking about you know. Goodbye Sidney, Susie and Mr and Mrs Robin. It was good to see you again, and as for you Sammy, well done for being so thoughtful and kind, but do try not to sleep through Christmas Day again next year!'

Sammy gave a little grin and looked down at his feet. 'I'll try, Santa.'

Information about our native Red Squirrel

Did you know that a squirrel's nest is really called a drey?

Did you know that squirrels are what are known as omnivores? That means they can eat plants, insects and lots of things you wouldn't really expect. In the wild, they eat tender leaf buds, wild fruits, nuts and acorns, bird eggs, seed crops, or even tree bark, and wild mushrooms

Where Red Squirrels live in Britain

There are just a few areas remaining where the red squirrel can be found in England, these being Northumberland, Brownsea Island in Dorset, and the Lake District.

For this reason, I have set this story in Dumfries and Galloway, Scotland, where I used to live. Of course, they are fairly widespread in other regions of Scotland, and they can be found in Northern Ireland and Wales.

It is generally thought that areas with pine trees are the favoured habitat of the Red Squirrel. However, this is more because the Grey Squirrel prefers other types of woodland, and therefore pine woodlands are more of a sanctuary to the Red Squirrel which is now one of our endangered species.